This book aligned with the Next Generation Science Standards (NGSS). The Next Generation Science Standards (NGSS) are reproduced with permission from the Department of Education.

By Aysha Imtiaz, Jake Hunter, Beth Hunter, Grant Cowell, and Bella Hunter.

Plants Need Water and Sunlight: Aditson's Three Sisters

Student Edition

ISBN 978-1-952346-46-0

STEMTaught® **Grade 2**
Next Generation Science

Ecosystems: Interactions, Energy, and Dynamics 2-LS2-1: Plan and conduct an investigation to determine if plants need sunlight and water to grow.

Jake Hunter
Mechanical Engineer
STEMTaught, California

Would you like to grow a garden with corn, beans, and squash like the ancient Native Americans did? Get ready to sprout some seeds in this STEMTaught Unit! I traveled to the Four Corners area of the United States to speak to my Navajo uncle about the Native American story of the "Three Sisters" and I am very excited to share what I learned with you!

Lesson Anchor
Soak a bean in water

A dry seed is a very patient thing. Seeds can wait a very long time before they begin to grow. They can wait years and years in a safe, dry spot and when you add water, the seed will sprout and begin to grow.

Find out what happens to a bean when you put it in water.

What you need:
- A bean and some water
- 1 Tedros test tube
- 1 pair of Toby tweezers
- 1 Mezzie measuring tape
- 1 Pippi pipette

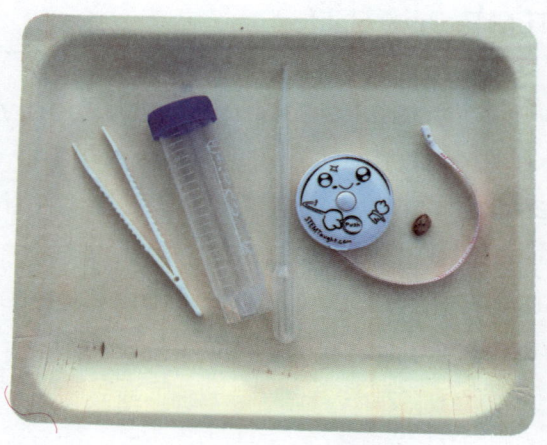

What you will do:

Observe and describe a dry bean seed. Soak your bean in water for an hour or more. Describe how your bean changes.

1. **Measure the length and width of your dry bean**

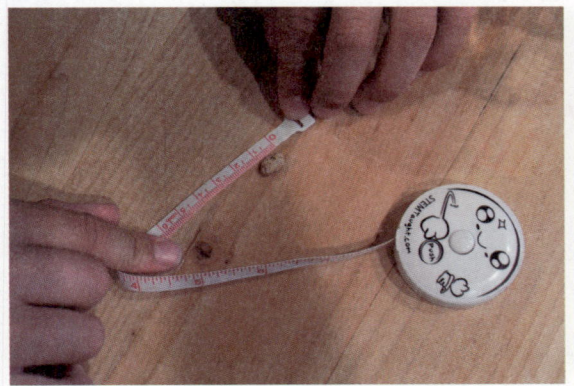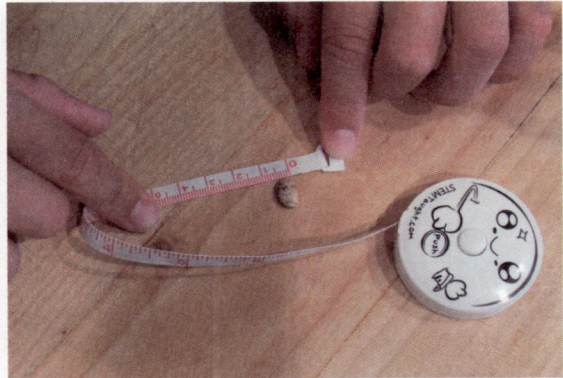

Use Mezzie measuring tape to measure your bean in millimeters.

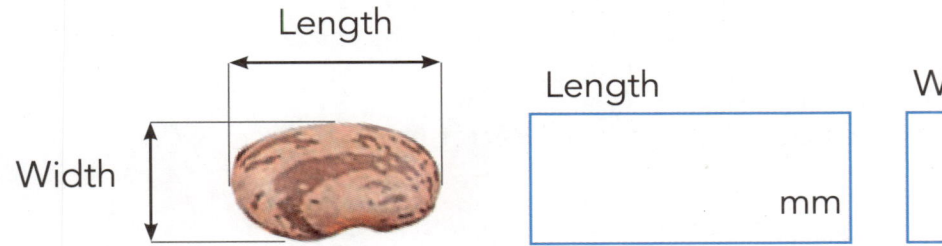

Length

Width

Length	Width
mm	mm

2. **Put your bean in water**

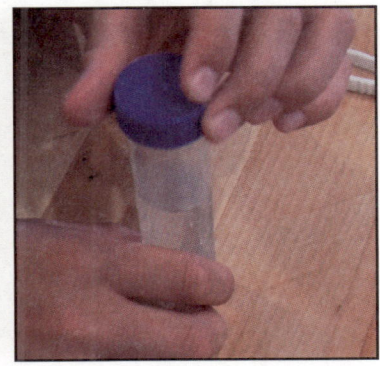

Fill Tedros test tube with water.

Put your bean in the water.

Put the cap on Tedros test tube.

3. Wait for an hour or more

Let your bean soak in the water for about an hour. Then go outside and dump out the water and bring your bean back to your desk.

1 hr

4 Measure the length and width of the wet bean.

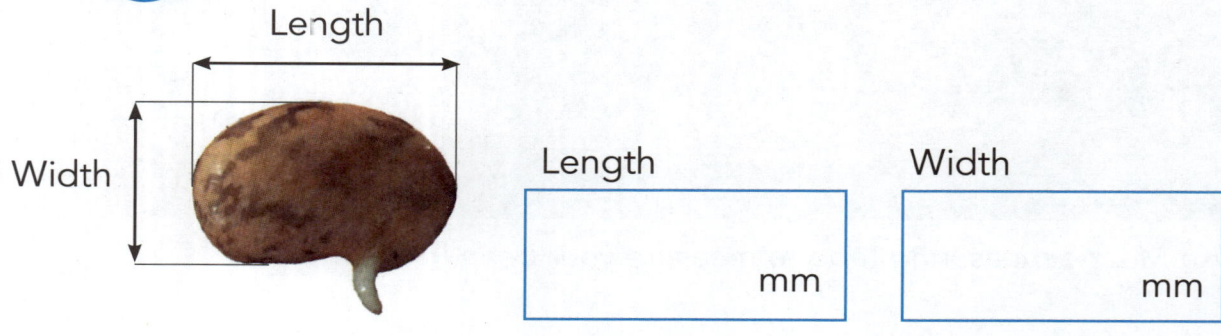

Length

Width

Length	Width
mm	mm

How did your bean change when you soaked it in water?

_____

_____

_____

_____

_____

_____

Can you explain it?

What do plants need to grow?

Think, Pair, Share!

What do you think plants need to grow?

_____

_____

_____

_____

_____

_____

Draw and label things that plants need to grow.

Plants give us what we need

Plants are beautiful and lovely. They are helpful for the environment and give us food to eat, shelter to keep us safe, flowers to smell and fresh air to breathe. Plants also provide shelter and food to animals.

Growing a garden helps this family live a healthy and happy life.

What things do we use that come from plants?

Think, Pair, Share!

Look around you! What things can you see that come from plants?

_____

_____

Draw and label things that come from plants

Most importantly, plants breathe out what we breathe in—meaning they take our carbon dioxide and give us oxygen in return, which helps keep us alive.

Seeds can wait a long time to grow

Plants start out as seeds, but the seeds don't sprout into a plant while sitting in a seed packet or on a dry table. A seed can't sprout until it has the things it needs to grow.

The Native Seeds SEARCH organization visits Native American tribes to preserve seeds from the crops they have been growing for hundreds of years.

Could a seed grow inside your tummy?

If you've ever accidentally eaten a watermelon seed, you might have thought that watermelons might start growing out of your ears. Or maybe you'd grow a huge watermelon inside of you.

We all know that would not happen. Your tummy doesn't have the things inside that a plant needs to grow.

Do you think a watermelon seed could grow inside your tummy? Why or why not?

_____

_____

_____

Seeds need water to help them sprout

Plants need certain things to grow. All living things, including plants, need water to survive. Almost 60% of the human body is made of water, and plants are made up of almost 90% water! Seeds need water to help them sprout.

This Navajo woman plants seeds in the dry desert and gives them water.

A dry seed can only sprout when water helps soften the hard outer covering and causes the seed to swell.

What will happen to a dry bean when you soak it in water?

Think, Pair, Share!

It's time to sprout some seeds!

You will get to do an experiment to see how well plants can grow with and without sunlight and water. It takes time to sprout a seed, so let's get started! Your seeds will be soaking up water while you are making your experimental plan. Before long, they will be ready to sprout and come to life.

What you need:

- Some beans (at least 4)

- 1 paper cup

- 1 pair of Toby tweezers (optional)

- 1 Pippi pipette (optional)

- 1 napkin or paper towel

What you will do:

First, place your beans on a napkin and get it wet. Then, roll the wet napkin and place it in a cup. Keep your napkin moist as you wait for your beans to sprout over the next week.

Design an experiment

Plants need certain things to grow. Can you design an experiment to discover if plants need water and light to grow? Use your STEMTaught skills! Work with a group to plan an experiment.

Find an answer to the question:

Do plants need water and light to grow?

Grow plants with and without water and light.

	Water	Light
Plant 1: Grown with water and sunlight		
Plant 2: Grown with water but without sunlight		
Plant 3: Grown without water but with sunlight		
Plant 4: Grown without water or sunlight		

In your groups, think of ways to do your experiment. Write down your plan on the next page.

My Baby Plant
Experimental Design Plan

Does a plant need water?

Does a plant need light?

Collecting Evidence

How will we measure our plants' growth at the end of the experiment?

_____

_____

_____

_____

Investigation plan

What type of plants will we use? _____

How much water will we give our plants for the water/no water test?

_____

_____

_____

_____

My Baby Plant
Experimental Design Plan

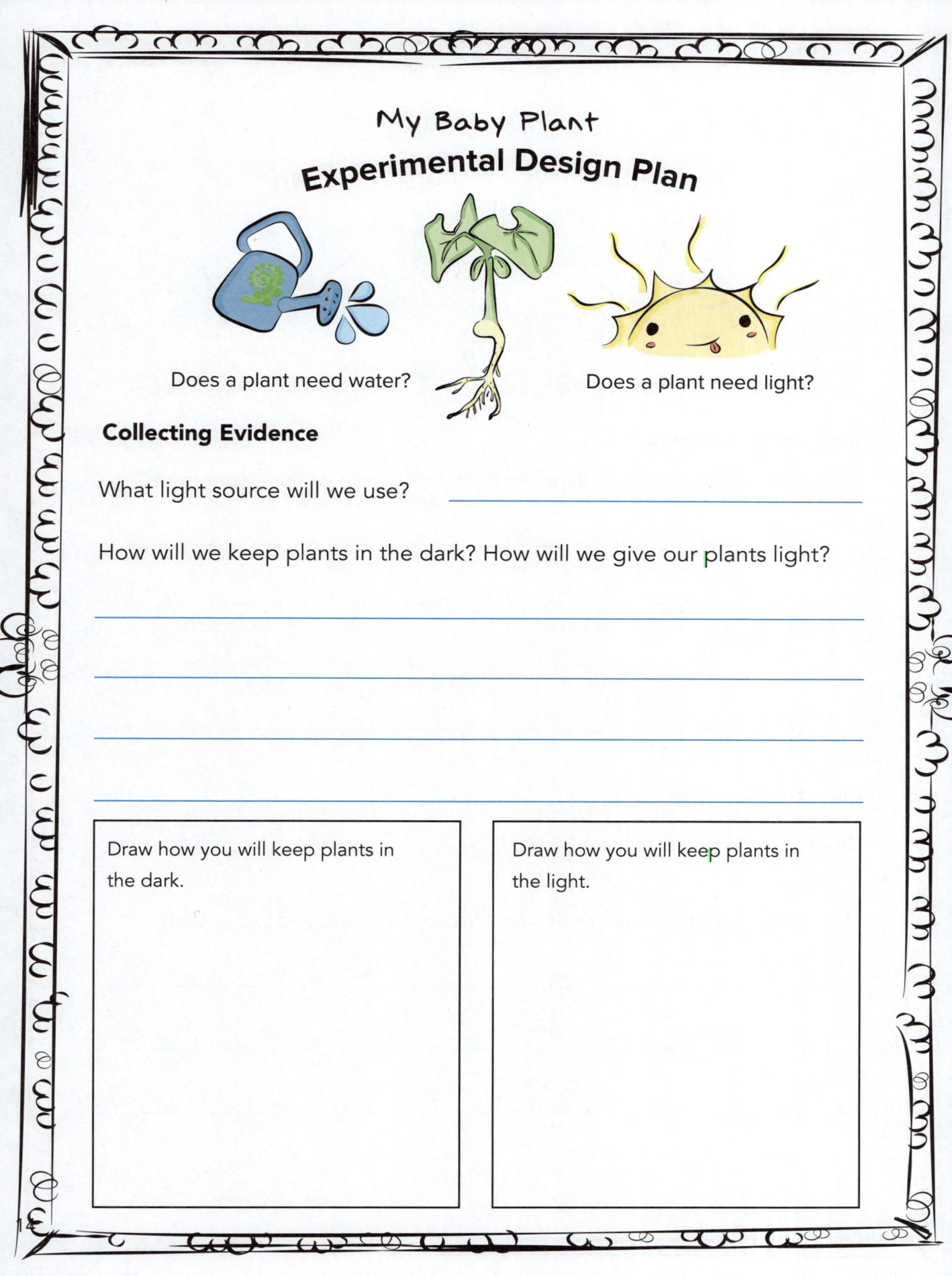

Does a plant need water?

Does a plant need light?

Collecting Evidence

What light source will we use? _____

How will we keep plants in the dark? How will we give our plants light?

_____

_____

_____

_____

Draw how you will keep plants in the dark.	Draw how you will keep plants in the light.

Experimental Results

Record your observations of each plant's growth. After your experiment share what you learned in a short presentation.

Draw and describe how each plant grew in your experiment

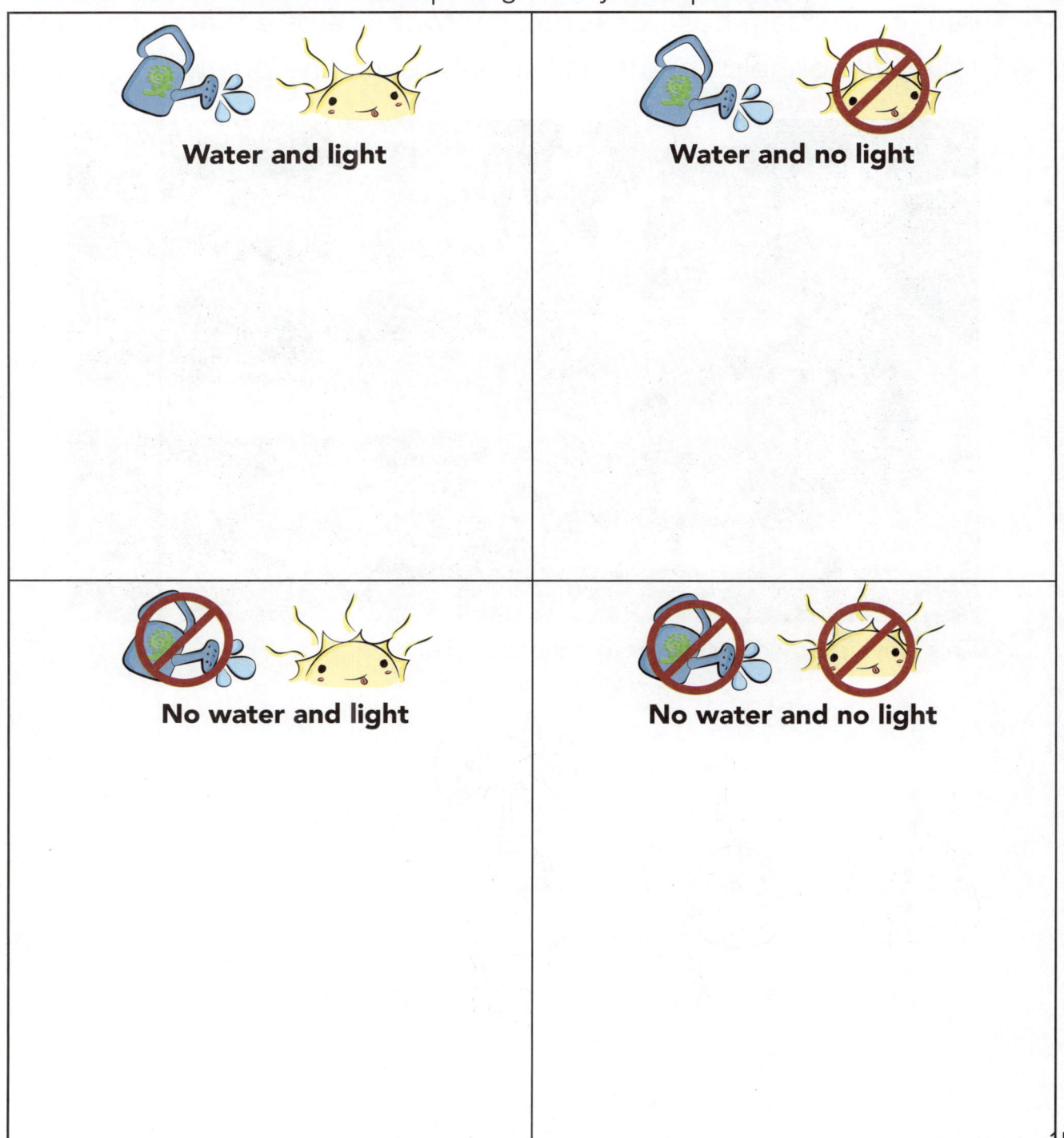

Water and light

Water and no light

No water and light

No water and no light

Plants need water to help them grow

When a seed sprouts it begins to grow leaves and roots. Instead of 'feeding' plants, we water them. There are many ways to water a plant! You could use a test tube, watering can, coffee can, hose or sprinkler. Water helps a plant grow taller. Water helps nutrients travel through the plant.

This Navajo boy gives water to his plants daily.

Plants take in water through their roots

Water in soil is absorbed through a plant's roots. The plant uses water to survive. The water also carries dissolved nutrients and minerals from the soil into the plant. Water vapor leaves the plant through its leaves in a process called transpiration.

This girl also gives water to the plants in her garden daily.

Plants lose water through their leaves

In growing plants, water is continuously evaporating from its leaves. A plant can lose many gallons or liters of water every day through transpiration.

You can observe transpiration

Even though leaves look and feel dry, moisture slowly but constantly comes out of leaves.

What you need:

- A clear plastic bag
- A piece of string, a rubber band, or twisty tie
- A plant

What you will do:

Make observations to see if you can see the moisture that comes out of the leaves of a plant.

Step 1: Seal a plastic bag over the leaves of a living plant.

Step 2: Leave it in sunlight for an hour to see what happens.

Describe the changes that you see. What happened inside the bag?

_____

_____

_____

Draw before and after: Draw what you observed

A plant with water stands upright, tall, proud and happy. A plant without water looks droopy and sad.

Plants use air, water, and sunlight

Plants also use sunlight in a process called Photosynthesis. 'Photo' means light, and 'synthesis' means to put together. Plants make their own food from air and water using sunlight.

In a dry desert with little moisture, this Navajo woman waters her plants with precious water using a coffee can.

What three things does a plant need for photosynthesis?

_____

_____

What does a plant make using photosynthesis?

_____

_____

IT'S SONG TIME!

Get ready to sing a song about what plants need! Sing these verses to the tune of **"Frere Jaques."**

What Plants Need!

Plants need sunlight, plants need sunlight

Yes they do! Yes they do!

Sunlight, air and water! Sunlight, air and water!

Make their food, make their food

Plants need air, plants need air

Yes they do! Yes they do!

Sunlight, air and water! Sunlight, air and water!

Make their food, make their food

Plants need water, plants need water

Yes they do! Yes they do!

Sunlight, air and water! Sunlight, air and water!

Make their food, make their food

Meet "The Three Sisters"

The story of "The Three Sisters" describes the farming techniques of the ancient Native American people. The three sisters are Corn, Bean, and Squash. The Native Americans talk very fondly of the three sisters. They respect them and call them "Junhuqua," meaning 'Our Sustainers'. They think of the sisters as if they were people with different talents and personalities.

Navajo Tail Corn

Sister Corn

Corn is the oldest sister. Her cornstalk stands tall and strong. She is very caring, responsible, and very important. She watches over her younger sisters, Bean and Squash.

Anasazi Bean

Sister Bean

Bean is very shy. Bean clings to Corn's stalk and peeks out from behind. The climbing bean plant grows up the corn stalk like a trellis. Although Bean is a bit shy, she is still a happy and playful younger sister.

Navajo Cushaw (Tail Squash)

Sister Squash

Squash is the youngest and the naughtiest sister. She crawls on the ground and is always making messes and getting into trouble. She is a lot to take care of for poor sister Corn, but you will see that she also helps Corn and Bean in a very important way.

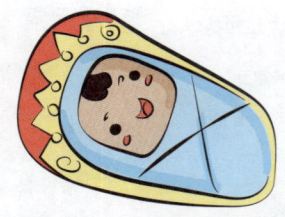

ADITSON'S THREE SISTERS

Part 1
Aditson is Born

Once upon a time, there was a gentle and wise little boy. As a small baby, his mother said, "His talent will be listening." For this reason, she named him Aditson, which means 'listener.' Aditson could hear things that nobody else could.

He heard the buzzing of the bees as they flew from flower to flower. He could hear the yucca plants as they competed to see who had the spikiest leaves. He even heard the twitch of the rabbit's whiskers as she sniffed the wind, and the flick of the deer's tail as she raised it proudly in the air.

Color the loom.

As Aditson grew, he learned to grow crops like his father, and soon, he had a small patch of land that was all his own.

His father told him, "Aditson, I know that you hear things that nobody else can hear. When you are farming, listen to what the plants have to tell you! They will tell you their secrets."

Aditson heard his father's words, as he always did. He also heard the poetry of the clouds, the whisper of the tall grass and the heartbeat of the warm soil. He was one with it all.

Aditson knew that his field was small and that it wouldn't feed the whole tribe, but he would do his best to grow his crops well. He dreamed of corn bread, blue corn loaf and three sister's stew.

*Color the
barrel cactus
and the bird.*

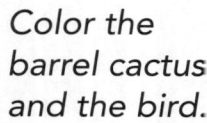

Aditson's tribe lived off the land. Three crops helped them live well—these crops were corn, beans and squash. With these three simple crops, all the members of the tribe could create feasts together.

They called these three crops 'Junhuqua,' meaning, 'Our Sustainers.' Everyone thought of the three crops as three sisters that cared for each other, as well as the tribe. Aditson's tribe sang songs to thank the Three Sisters for their harvest.

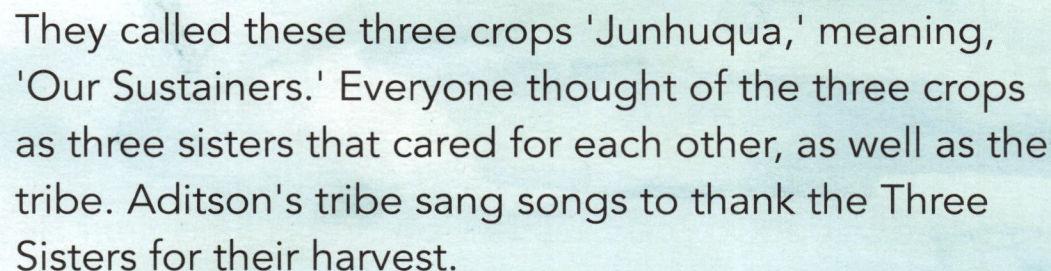

Part 2

Sister Corn

Aditson decided to plant Sister Corn in his field first. He planted many corn seeds close together so he would have lots of corn. He carried buckets of water from the stream, and gave Corn all the water she could ever want.

A few days later, newly sprouted corn was poking up out of the field. It covered the field like a thick, soft carpet of grass. Aditson eagerly ran to listen to Sister Corn. To his surprise, he didn't hear the praise he had expected. Instead, he heard her disappointment.

There's water all over! It covers my feet!
I can't stand—it's too crowded, there's not enough heat.
The soil's not rich, and that I regret.
I wish it was moist, not squishy and wet.
There's not enough drainage, I can't give a good crop.
When all I can feel is this drip and this drop!

Corn was true to her word and Aditson did not have a good crop that season.

Why is Sister Corn unhappy?

Think, Pair, Share!

Color the mice.

Aditson knew exactly how to make Sister Corn happy the next growing season. To keep her roots drier, he dug up the earth to make mounds. He helped Corn grow tall and glorious. The Sun's light warmed the mounds. Now, puddles of water only formed between the mounds, where Corn's roots would not get too wet.

Sister Corn grew well that year, and everyone in the village praised Aditson for his plentiful harvest, but Aditson knew that Corn was still not happy.

When Aditson went away, she was upset and called out to him, "Aditson! Come back! It's so boring when you are away!"

Aditson spent many days and nights keeping Sister Corn company, but he could not stay in his field all the time. Aditson did not know how he could keep Corn from being lonely when he was gone.

Think, Pair, Share!

How did the mounds help keep Corn's roots dry?

Wow, he's good!

Color the critters.

Part 3

Sister Bean

Aditson's father was proud of his son. The next season, he gave Aditson another field.

"Now, you can plant your second sister, Bean, in your new field."

Aditson knew this was a mark of honor. He worked equally hard for his second sister, Bean. He carefully pulled weeds, and made mounds. To his surprise, when Bean sprouted, he heard sadness, not celebration!

My beanstalk tipped over, it rests on the ground
The birds and the insects hover around
I'm dry and I'm thirsty, there's not enough drink
I'm too far from the water, that's what I think!
Oh, Dear, I'm so shy. I feel so exposed
I need someone to hold me, to share all my woes!

Aditson tried his best to keep the birds and insects away from Sister Bean. He realized that he hadn't given Bean what she needed.

Why is Sister Bean unhappy?

Think, Pair, Share!

During the day, Aditson kept Bean and Corn company and he was getting very tired.

As Bean grew, she flopped down on the ground because she did not have any support to help her stand up straight and tall. Sister Corn drooped down— for lack of a friend. Aditson had a brilliant idea!

He planted Bean next to Corn on the same mound. Bean had an older sister to cling to. Bean grew up Corn's strong stalk and felt safe.

Corn was not lonely anymore. Having sister Bean nearby made Corn feel fresh and nourished. Bean gave special nutrients to the soil. The two sisters no longer drooped, they both stood tall and proud.

Think, Pair, Share!

How does Corn help Bean grow?
How does Bean help Corn grow?

Color and draw some insects of your own.

Aditson was happy, but his body was tired because he pulled weeds constantly. He felt overwhelmed. He sat on a rock and chanted:

> *Junhuqua, my Sustainers and grace*
> *I will keep you both happy*
> *Your growing season won't go to waste*
> *It's my duty and privilege, to tend to you so ...*
> *... even though weak and tired I grow*

Aditson's parents were concerned because he seemed so tired. Corn and Bean were also concerned, but Aditson said he was alright. He would rest for a bit, before going back to tend to his crops.

He only let himself complain when nobody could hear—at least, he thought nobody could hear ...

Part 4

Sister Squash

Little Squash, who grew near Aditson's field, was listening. She could see how tired Aditson was and she wanted to help. She waved her broad, flat leaves to get his attention.

"Here! Down here!" she squeaked.

Squash was known for being little and naughty. She grew out in many different directions in a messy and disorganized fashion. Aditson had heard about her mischief before.

Aditson bent down to hear what she had to say.

"You always work too hard!" she began. "You are a good farmer, but you must let me help you. Promise me that you will plant me with my Sisters next growing season! Plant our seeds near each other and you will see how I can help them."

Aditson agreed and made a promise to honor Sister Bean's wish.

In the next growing season, Aditson kept his promise. He planted Corn, Bean and Squash together. Corn grew high above the mound and Bean grew happily up her stalk. Squash spread her broad, flat leaves out all over the ground below. Her leaves shaded the ground so weeds could not grow. Squash wasn't naughty, she was actually very helpful.

Together, The Three Sisters grew, taller, stronger, and happier than ever before. Aditson was finally able to rest!

What did Sister Squash do to help?

Think, Pair, Share!

Color the yucca, deer and bees.

Word of Aditson and his remarkable garden spread throughout the land. Soon, other farmers and tribes started growing Corn, Bean and Squash together on small mounds, just like Aditson.

Using this farming technique the land gave them much more food.

From that day on, the Native Americans always grew the Three Sisters together, all thanks to Aditson who listened to his special friends—Corn, Bean and Squash.

Why did the farmers grow more food using Aditson's method?

Think, Pair, Share!

Mmm ... Yummy!

The Three Sisters help each other

Native Americans experimented to figure out something years ago that science has also confirmed. The fact that the Three Sisters grew well together is not just a story. The Three Sisters play very important roles in helping each other grow.

Can you spot corn, bean and squash plants growing together in this photo?

Think, Pair, Share!

Sister Bean: A bean plant gives out nitrogen from its roots, which is an important nutrient that all plants need. Bean provides natural fertilizer for Corn and Squash.

Sister Corn: Corn provides a stalk for the climbing bean plant.

Sister Squash: Squash has broad flat leaves that block sunlight and stop low lying weeds from growing.

Grow corn, beans and squash at home

Now that you know how to care for plants, you can be like Aditson! Plant the Three Sisters at home.

Prepare your seed packet:

1. Cut out your seed packet and fold on the dotted lines.

2. Glue the side and bottom tab down to make your seed packet.

3. Put corn, bean and squash seeds inside your packet.

4. Glue the top tab down to seal your packet.

The Three Sisters
Sister Corn, Bean, and Squash

I ♡ STEM Tot®

Fold and glue

Fold and glue

Growing Instructions: Make a mound of dirt. Plant your corn, beans and squash 6 inches apart. Place the seeds in holes that are about 1 inch deep.

STEM Tot®

Three Sisters Stew

- 2 cups corn

- 2 cups diced squash

- 2 cups beans

- 1 onion

Soak the corn and beans overnight if dry. Add meat, squash, onions, water and spices such as salt, sage, and paprika. Simmer for two hours.

How do Bean and Corn help each other?

_____

_____

_____

_____

_____

How do the mounds help keep Corn's roots moist but not too wet?

_____

_____

_____

_____

_____

What did Squash do to help everyone?

_____

_____

_____

_____

Explain the Phenomanon

Draw a picture to help you explain what you learned in this unit.

STEM Tot®

What do plants need to survive?

Explain the
Phenomenon